Packing Your
Spiritual Suitcase

Pamela M. Torres
&
Brenda Keyes Granfield

WestBow
PRESS
A DIVISION OF THOMAS NELSON

WestBow Press books may be ordered through booksellers or by contacting:

WestBow Press
A Division of Thomas Nelson
1663 Liberty Drive
Bloomington, IN 47403
www.westbowpress.com
1-(866) 928-1240

ISBN: 978-1-4497-0663-0 (sc)
ISBN: 978-1-4497-0664-7 (dj)
ISBN: 978-1-4497-0746-0 (e)

Library of Congress Control Number: 2010938924

Printed in the United States of America

WestBow Press rev. date: 11/10/10

— Contents —

— Introduction —

My name is Pamela M. Torres. I am not a pastor. I have not been to seminary or college to study the Holy Scriptures. I have been a Christian and a follower of the Lord Jesus since January 8,1970. I have studied and been in church all of those years. But, I am not a professional *church person*, just an ordinary woman, who God has chosen to give this message to. I hope your lives will be impacted as much as mine has been by this concept.

Not all of you will **get** this concept. The Lord has already shown me that. But, **IF** you do **get** it, this book could change your whole outlook on the way you live your life. I pray that the Lord will guide you through this and help you discover your inner talents, so that you can accomplish something great for the Lord!

I'll bet you are wondering, where did she get this idea? The Holy Spirit gave this book to me as I stood in my husband's room at ***Hope Hospice*** shortly before he died. I was praying over his bed. The nurses had told me I had to say goodbye. As I was trying to do the impossible task ahead of me, the Holy Spirit spoke to me and through Him I said, "Eddie, honey, it's almost time to go. Have you got your suitcase all packed and ready to go? Do you have all your memories of your brothers and sisters in there? How about the memories of those that you have led to the Lord? Do you have all your memories of you and I?" His sister was on the other side of the bed looking at me like I had flipped out and lost what was left of my mind.

But, while I was saying that, the Lord told me that I was to write this in a book. He gave me the illustrations. He gave me the original concept. He has given me the courage to take on this project. He has given me the strength to walk the *widow walk,* with Him right there beside me, urging me on, and encouraging me to take another step when I have wanted to stop, curl up into a ball and wait for life to pass me by.

Do you remember when a boss would call his secretary in, to his office, and he would dictate a letter or correspondence? That is exactly how I felt, as in my spirit I could see the Lord sitting next to me telling everything to write. He would give me a sentence to write and I would type it. Then, He would give me the next sentence to type. He waited on me to finish, before continuing. That is how inspired this book is.

Enjoy this book and then pass it on to a friend. Prepare yourself to experience the Glory of God and see, when you walk with Him, anything is possible. Anything!

DEDICATION PAGE

This book is dedicated to my late husband
Germany Eddie Torres
Born July 24, 1950 ------ Died June 29, 2008

Eddie was what you might call a high maintenance kind of guy. He required every moment I could give him. He had tons more clothes than I did. His hair had to be just so and when we first met he had at least twenty pairs of shoes. But, wow, what a wonderful man he was! He lived right on the edge, all the time, not afraid of what life might throw at him and it threw him some curve balls more than once.

As I watched his physical beauty fade, little by little, his strong inner beauty was revealed more and more, like a beacon, on a starless night. He was a strong man in every sense of the word, emotionally, physically, and most important, spiritually. He loved the Lord Jesus and together we told as many people as possible about the Lord. I have never seen a person work harder. He lived to work and serve Jesus, and to love. He had a huge heart to help others and his *Spiritual Suitcase* was bulging by the time he was at death's door. He witnessed to every nurse, doctor or orderly he saw. His testimony is recorded at the end of this book.

I will never know another person like my Eddie. He was a truly unique individual, who I love with all my heart. I only wish I could have been a better wife and have shown him exactly how much I loved him.

THE DEDICATION PAGE

BRENDA K. GRANFIELD
AND
LARRY L. GRANFIELD

I want to especially thank my sister and brother in law, for all of their unselfish dedication to me and my late husband. Without hesitation, they put their own lives on hold, to help us out, while Eddie was at home, in the hospital in Fort Myers, or in the hospital in Gainesville. Brenda never quit praying with us or quoting scriptures to encourage us. They put up their own money when ours ran low or when the insurance company and other people started hassling us about money. I would never have made it through this journey if they and the Lord Jesus had not been right there with me. Thank God for giving me this sister and brother in law!

II TIMOTHY 4:7 KJV: *"I HAVE FOUGHT A GOOD FIGHT, I HAVE FINISHED MY COURSE, I HAVE KEPT THE FAITH."*

PSALM 37:4 KJV: *"DELIGHT THYSELF ALSO IN THE LORD; AND HE SHALL GIVE THEE THE DESIRES OF THINE HEART."*

MATTHEW 6:19-21 NIV: *"DO NOT STORE UP FOR YOURSELVES TREASURES ON EARTH, WHERE MOTH AND RUST DESTROY, AND WHERE THIEVES BREAK IN AND STEAL. BUT STORE UP FOR YOURSELVES TREASURES IN HEAVEN,---FOR WHERE YOUR TREASURE IS, THERE YOUR HEART WILL BE ALSO."*

MATTHEW 12:36-37 NIV:
"BUT I TELL YOU THAT MEN WILL HAVE TO GIVE ACCOUNT ON THE DAY OF JUDGMENT FOR EVERY CARELESS WORD THEY HAVE SPOKEN. FOR BY YOUR WORDS YOU WILL BE ACQUITTED, AND BY YOUR WORDS YOU WILL BE CONDEMNED."

ROMANS 12:11 NKJV: *"…NOT LAGGING IN DILIGENCE, FERVENT IN SPIRIT, SERVING THE LORD."*

PACKING YOUR SPIRITUAL SUITCASE

I want to start by having you imagine an open suitcase laying on your bed. It is old and tattered, but still sturdy. In the back, is a pouch that can be detached, if you want. What are you going to put in your suitcase? If you were going on an extended journey, you would need to pack your suitcase carefully, so you wouldn't forget anything.

So, it is, as we go through life, we are packing our *Spiritual Suitcase* for our eventual journey to the next life.

What are you packing in your *Spiritual Suitcase*?

Let's say, you are going on a long excursion. You will need to pack a suitcase to take with you. An extra pair of comfortable walking shoes, with good tight laces, or a sweater, in case the weather turns chilly, a good book to read, on the train, or an extra pair of glasses, just in case, you break or lose yours. You would check and double check to make sure that you had your ticket ready and close at hand. Depending on your destination, you may need a hat to keep the sun out of your eyes or perhaps a good pair of sunglasses, not the inexpensive drug store ones, and sunscreen. You will need a change of clothes, some for leisure times and some for dressing up. A nice pair of slacks with a jacket and polished shoes, that will give you a finished look. You will want to ensure that you have plenty of your medications. Do you need to go to the pharmacy before departing?

Just as you would be very specific about what you would pack for an extended trip, even more so, we must be very careful about what we pack in our *spiritual suitcase* for our eventual trip to the next life. The Egyptians filled their tombs with luxurious, physical items, to take with them to the after life. They believed they could take it all with them, but, in actuality, all we can take with us is our spiritual wealth.

NOTES

CHAPTER ONE

Packing Your Spiritual Wealth
Packing Faith In Jesus

What is spiritual wealth? It's accumulation of those precious ones you have led to the Lord, the words you have read and memorized from the Word of God, the Bible, the special times you have spent praising and worshiping the Lord Jesus, the good deeds you have done for others, as unto the Lord, the work you have done for God, all such acts are spiritual wealth. But, your most important spiritual wealth is your faith in Jesus, as your Lord and personal Savior.

When "packing" the tools necessary for your spiritual journey, your faith is the first thing you need to pack. It must be packed on the bottom and in the middle of your suitcase, so that you will have a good, solid foundation, to pack other things on top of.

THIS SOLID FOUNDATION THAT YOU NEED IS A STRONG BELIEF IN JESUS CHRIST, AS YOUR LORD AND PERSONAL SAVIOR.

I Corinthians 3:10-11 NIV: *"By the grace God has given me, I laid a foundation as an expert builder, and someone else is* *building on it. ---For no one can lay any foundation other than the one already laid, which is Jesus Christ."*

If you've ever traveled, the first thing you usually need to do is to make your reservation. In order to do this **you have to know where you are going.** Unlike a vacation destination, where the choices are endless, when it comes to your spiritual destination you only have two choices, **Heaven or Hell**. By not choosing, during your lifetime, the decision will be made for you, by default. When you accept Jesus into your life and pack Him in your *spiritual suitcase*, by faith, you **simultaneously** pack your destination of Heaven!

Visualize again, the open suitcase, sitting on your bed. As we've already discussed **your faith and destination are the most important things you need to pack in your *spiritual suitcase.*** Without Jesus, nothing else will stick in your suitcase. He is the glue that holds it all together. He is the one who makes it possible to pack everything else you will be packing, as you travel on the road of life.

In order to apply faith, it's essential that you believe that Jesus is the Son of God. He died on the cross to pay the price, for your sins and mine. Everyone is a sinner therefore, we all need a Savior. Someone to cleanse us of **all** the wrong we have done. You know those bad thoughts or deeds that you don't want anyone else to know about, those obvious ones and even those sins that are not clear to anyone, but you and God. Who could possibly pay that price, so that we could go to Heaven when we die? **Only Jesus**, the Holy Son of Almighty God! In fact, Jesus was God in human form.

Several verses in the King James Version better clarify Jesus deity and purposes on this earth.

John 3:16-17: *"For God so loved the world, that He gave His only begotten Son, that whosoever believeth in Him should not perish, but have everlasting life. For God sent not His Son into the world to condemn the world; but that the world through Him might be saved."*

Romans 3:10-12 *"As it is written, There is none righteous, (good) no, not one: There is none that understandeth, there is none that seeketh after God. ----There is none that doeth good, no, not one."*

Romans 3:23: *"For all have sinned, and come short of the glory of God."*

Romans 6:23a: *"For the wages of sin is death -----"*

Hebrews 9:27-28: *"And as it is appointed unto men once to die, but after this the judgment: So Christ was once offered to bear the sins of many."*

BUT

Romans 5:8: *"But God commendeth His love toward us, in that, while we were yet sinners, Christ died for us."*

Romans 6:23b: *"But the gift of God is eternal life through Jesus Christ our Lord."*

Romans 10:13: *"For whosoever shall call upon the name of the Lord SHALL be saved."*

Acts 4:12: *"Neither is there salvation in any other: for there is none other name under Heaven given among men, where by we must be saved."*

Isaiah 1:18: *"though your sins be as scarlet, they shall be as white as snow; though they be red like crimson, they shall be as wool."*

If you don't know the Lord Jesus, as your Savior, you are not on your way to Heaven. **Thus your *Spiritual Suitcase* will be empty.** Faith in Jesus, is **the only way** to get you a one way ticket to Heaven. If you don't have your ticket ready and punched, you can't get on board the train to eternal life with the Lord. Do you know Him? Why, not place your trust in Him, now, for your eternal salvation?

Revelation 3:20 KJV: *"Behold, I stand at the door, and knock: if any man hear my voice, and open the door, I will come in to him, and will sup with him, and he with me."*

One day there will be a judgment. Are <u>you</u> covered in the blood of Jesus? Just pray this simple prayer and ask Him into your life, today and for all of eternity.

Dear Lord Jesus, I know that I am a sinner. But, I believe that You died on the cross, for the forgiveness of my sins. Please, come into my heart, right now, and forgive me of all my sins. I turn my life completely over to You and thank You for making a place for me in Heaven when I die, where I will reign with You forever, Amen.

With those words, the Lord Jesus is packed in your ***spiritual suitcase*** forever! Welcome to a beautiful new spiritual journey.

NOTES

— CHAPTER TWO —

Interpretation Of The First Illustration

Let's go back to the illustration, you read earlier, about the long excursion.

The Lord offers an interpretation, of that illustration, so pray that Jesus will reveal to you the personal application for your life. Here are some keys to preparing for this journey.

Let's say you are going on a long excursion:

1. Excursion refers to your mission for Christ.
2. It will not be a quick trip.
3. An excursion is an adventure that has many challenges along the way.
4. It will not be an easy road.
5. There will be troubles and hardships, but at the end, you will realize it has all been worth everything, you have had to endure, to get to your Heavenly destination.
6. Your guide on this excursion, is the Lord Jesus. He goes first, to make sure you have a safe road to travel on.

An extra pair of comfortable walking shoes, with good tight laces:

1. Jesus is our firm foundation. If you don't have that, you will slip and fall, just like a good pair of shoes grips the ground so you will be safe.
2. You have to feel comfortable in your mission for God. It has to be a good fit for you, just like your favorite shoes.
3. The good tight laces means safety and security which is found only in the Lord Jesus. He is our safety net.
4. Don't let the devil trip you up.
5. You have to be secure in your knowledge of God's word and His love for you and all mankind.
6. We are **bound** in the Spirit of the Lord, just like the laces keep the shoes tightly on your feet, the Holy Spirit lives in us and keeps us tightly bound with Christ and on the straight and narrow path. Psalms 147:3 and Acts 20:22.

Matthew 7:13-14 NIV: *"Enter through the narrow gate. For wide is the gate and broad is the road that leads to destruction, and many enter through it. But small is the gate and narrow the road that leads to life, and only a few find it."*

7. Loose laces represents a sloppy, unprepared life, not pulled tight in the Word and not filled with the Holy Spirit, thus making you sloppy in your study of God's Word and your prayer life.

A sweater, in case the weather turns chilly:

1. Be prepared for the unexpected.
2. It won't be an easy ride.
3. There will be adversities. The winds may be cold, because everyone will not be accepting of you or the message you are bringing. Hang in there! Don't give up! Jesus is right there with you.

Hebrews 13:5 KJV: *"I will never leave thee, nor forsake thee."*

A good book to read on the train:

1. Enjoy the ride! Enjoy the small pleasures of life.
2. Be careful what you put into your mind.

An extra pair of glasses, just in case:

1. Be prepared and plan ahead.
2. Keep your eyes on Christ, not this world.
3. If there is sin in your life, you can't see Jesus clearly.

Psalm 25:15 NIV: *"My eyes are ever on the Lord, for only He will release my feet from the snare."*

4. You need to focus on the path Jesus has you on, so that you don't trip up and fall into sin. Keep your eyes open.
5. Look for the opportunities that Jesus is leading you into.

Check and double check that you have your ticket ready:

1. Jesus is your ticket to Heaven. .
2. Stay on target! Don't get side tracked!

I Corinthians 9:24 & 26 NIV: *"Do you not know that in a race all the runners run, but only one gets the prize? Run in such a way as to get the prize.---Therefore I do not run like a man running aimlessly."*

John 14:6 NIV: *"I am the way and the truth and the life. No one comes to the Father except through me."*

You may need a hat to keep the sun out of your eyes--sunglasses --sunscreen:

1. Be prepared for anything, by putting on as much of the Word of God as you can, like the sunscreen.

Ephesians 6:13 &17 NIV: *"Therefore put on the full armor of God, so that when the day of evil comes, you may be able to stand your ground, and after you have done everything, to stand. ---Take the helmet of salvation and the sword of the Spirit, which is the Word of God."*

I Peter 5:8 KJV: *"Be sober, be vigilant; because your adversary the devil,-- walketh about, seeking whom he may devour."*

I Peter 5:9 NIV: *"Resist him, standing firm in the faith."*

2. The hat, sunglasses and sunscreen are a representation of the way the Lord protects us from the world and watches out for us.

Psalm121:5 & 8 NIV: *"The Lord watches over you---the Lord is your shade at your right hand. The Lord will watch over your coming and going both now and forever more."*

Not the inexpensive drug store ones:

1. Don't take the easy way.
2. Don't skimp on what you give back to the Lord. Don't do the job halfway and expect to get full pay. Don't give God your leftovers. Don't say, 'that's good enough' when you have done a halfway job or hurried through, just to get done. Give the job the time it requires, not rushing through and doing a bad job. You won't be giving God your best. The Jeff Ferguson song, **"Halfway" says:** *"He didn't halfway save us or halfway deliver us, He didn't halfway set our feet on the rock to stay."* Jesus

never gave us anything, but His very best. He deserves our very best.

3. You have to be willing to put in the time and effort to reach the desired results, such as studying and memorizing the Holy Word.

4. You need to make an investment, in your future with the Lord Jesus.

5. It takes time to be prepared to live for Jesus and to lead others to Him. Time to learn the verses, to memorize them and to be able to find them, quickly, in the Bible. Time spent in diligent prayer, praying for others and that the Lord will be with you and show you the right way.

II Timothy 2:15 KJV: *"Study to shew thyself approved unto God."*

Change of clothes, a finished look:

1. Put on the whole armor of God, Ephesians 6:10-17.

2. You need to put on your best when representing Jesus. Your appearance, that doesn't mean just your clothes, but also the way you act, can draw or turn people away from the Lord. Even when you are in leisure time, you must be prepared to tell others about Him. Be careful what you wear, dress modestly, in order to put on a good appearance for Christ.

3. You have to be prepared by, for example, buying and passing out clean, well kept gospel tracts, that aren't all wrinkled and dirty. What do people see when they see you? Are you just like everyone else, in your appearance, habits and language? Do you go to the same establishments? Do you listen to gossip and dirty jokes or wear provocative clothing like others do?

Philippians 1:27 NIV: *"Whatever happens, conduct yourselves in a manner worthy of the gospel of Christ."*

Ephesians 4:29 KJV: *"Let no corrupt communication proceed out of your mouth, but that which is good to the use of edifying, that it may minister grace unto the hearers."*

James 3:9-10 NIV: *"With the tongue we praise our Lord and Father, and with it we curse men, who have been made in God's likeness. Out of the same mouth come praise and cursing. My brothers, this should not be."*

James 1:26 NIV: *"If anyone considers himself religious and yet does not keep a tight rein on his tongue, he deceives himself and his religion is worthless."*

People are looking at you to be different, if you claim the name of Jesus. You can't tell others about the Lord in one breath and in the next, talk bad about the new employee or show up to work late, hung over from being out all night drinking or use every curse word known to man and expect them to turn towards the Lord. You are representing Jesus. Will they see Him in you? You are accountable, for every word you utter, every deed you do or don't do or even for what you think, Matthew 12:36-37. Thank God, we have Jesus to forgive us of all these sins.

James 1:8 KJV: *"A double minded man is unstable in all his ways."*

II Corinthians 6:17 -18 KJV: *"Wherefore come out from among them, and be ye separate, saith the Lord, and touch not the unclean thing; and I will receive you, And will be a Father unto you, and ye shall be my sons and daughters, saith the Lord Almighty."*

Give the Christian life your all! This is the most important decision anyone will ever make. It is your job to be ready, at all times, to show them the way. This may be their only chance. God has put you in this situation, for a reason, which may be to guide them towards the Lord. You may have to put your own plans on hold, in order to take the time to find out what the person's needs are and to show a true interest in their lives, before you will be able to lead them to the Lord.

Medications--pharmacy:

1. Jesus is our pharmacy. We can go to Him with any problem. He can solve them or bring us through them.
2. Medications means our daily Bible study and prayer. Just like you take a multi-vitamin every day to protect you against illness, so we need the strength and comfort we will find in the Bible, when times get tough.
3. He is there for us, no matter what we are going through, death, illness, financial burdens, unruly children or temptations. He is walking right there next to us. You need to pack your *spiritual suitcase* daily by living for Him.

Matthew 6:33 NIV: *"But seek first His Kingdom and his righteousness, and all these things will be given to you as well."*

John 10:10b KJV: *"I am come that they might have life, and that they might have it more abundantly."*

Just like a necessary medication, that you have to take every day to keep yourself healthy, you need daily Bible study and prayer time to keep you spiritually healthy. It is your Christian food. **Without it, you will starve**. Pack your *spiritual suitcase* daily with diligent prayer and Bible study.

You need to repent and confess your sins, daily. Only if you are clean, with no unconfessed sins, will you be totally effective, in your work for the Kingdom.

I John 1:9 KJV: *"If we confess our sins, He is faithful and just to forgive us our sins, and to cleanse us from all unrighteousness."*

NOTES

— CHAPTER THREE —

Packing Forgiveness: Passing On To the Final Destination

If you have a loved one, that is about to pass on, into eternity, you may need to help them finish packing their **spiritual suitcase**. The first thing you need to determine, is, do they know the Lord Jesus, without a shadow of a doubt, as their Lord and personal Savior? If not, lead them, to the Lord the same way I showed you in chapter one. Call any pastor of a Bible believing church or 1-888-need-him, or Jesus 20-20 on the internet, for help.

The next thing you need to help them pack, is forgiveness. You can pack it on the right side, of their suitcase; right next to their solid foundation, their faith in Jesus. It is important, that the dying person forgive anyone who has hurt them and ask forgiveness from anyone they have injured. This is in no way a determination of salvation. If they have accepted Jesus, as their Savior, they are saved and on their way to Heaven. But, if possible, they need to give and receive forgiveness.

As we waited for the inevitable, my husband's death, our families gathered together, putting aside our differences, for awhile, knowing that they would be picked up again later. As we waited, my oldest daughter brought in food, reminding us that life doesn't stop because a traumatic event was about to happen.

You know how it is, a misspoken word explodes into a landslide, of arguments and hurt feelings. Before you know it, years have passed, with each family member taking sides, not speaking or saying anything good about the other person; forgive and forget. This is impossible to do without God's help.

Luke 18:27 KJV: *"The things which are impossible with men are possible with God."*

Forgiveness is never easy to give or to receive. The scars can run so deep and the hurt so devastating, that it is nearly impossible to forgive, but you must try, for the dying person's sake. Only by giving and receiving forgiveness can the dying person have a clear conscience and not leave any unfinished business. They need to settle their accounts, as it were, **if at all possible** and sometimes, it isn't. Sometimes, a person passes unexpectedly. But, if you are just waiting, for the inescapable to happen, as in the case of a terminal patient, this is very important. After all, there will be no second chance to make things right.

My husband, Eddie, had unfinished business, but we didn't know for sure what it was. He could not speak, at all, towards the end. We started the guessing game, of sending in the likely suspects, to be alone with him. We thought maybe, it was me, his over-bearing wife. It wasn't. Maybe his one sister? No. Finally, his son arrived back at *Hope Hospice* and after spending time with his father, each giving forgiveness, in their own way, we determined my husband had been holding on until he spoke with his son, with whom he had always had a problematical relationship.

His son, Eddie Jr., had left, to get the tuxedo, he had worn at his wedding. When he returned, he ask me, (his step mother) if it would be alright if his father worn it to be buried in. They had made peace with each other.

It is extremely important, to remember, a fact that I did not know before this experience. The dying person, who may appear to be comatose, can hear you until the very end. Hearing is the last function to shut down. They just may not be able to respond. My husband squeezed my hand, as I laid in a recliner next to his bed. If you ask the person to forgive you, they can hear you.

Forgiveness, not easy to give or receive. But, the Bible says if we do not forgive, we will not be forgiven.

Mark 11:26 KJV: *"But if ye do not forgive, neither will your Father which is in Heaven forgive your trespasses."*

After all, the ultimate show of forgiveness was when the Lord Jesus died on the cross, suffering horrendous pain, all for the forgiveness of MY sins. An otherwise, worthless being, becomes the daughter of the Most High God by simply accepting His forgiveness for my countless sins. **I am clean once again! I am forgiven**! Are you? You can be. Just ask Jesus to forgive you, come into your heart and be your personal Savior. Turn your life over to Him and He **will** forgive you.

You will be adding to your *spiritual suitcase* by helping your loved one with their final challenge, in this life, forgiveness.

Luke 6:37 NIV: *"Do not judge, and you will not be judged. Do not condemn, and you will not be condemned. Forgive, and you will be forgiven."*

Luke 17:3 NIV: *"If your brother sins, rebuke him, and if he repents, forgive him. If he sins against you seven times in a day, and seven times comes back to you and says, 'I repent,' forgive him."*

Are you packing forgiveness in your own *spiritual suitcase?*

As we pass through life, we may inadvertently pack things we shouldn't have. Thus, the next concept we need to consider is the concept of unpacking. You should be packing things like, leading others to Jesus, helping someone in need, or forgiving someone who has done you wrong, Or unpacking things like, bitterness, being judgmental, anger, or unforgiveness, not just once in awhile, but every day of every year. Every day, you should be packing or unpacking your *spiritual suitcase.* You may need to help your loved one, unpack certain things from their suitcase.

How do we unpack our ***spiritual suitcases***? This is done only through much prayer.

1. Confess any known sin to the Lord.
2. Pray that God will reveal any unconfessed sin to you.
3. Pray and ask God to forgive you of all your sins.
4. Be in the Word daily, so you will see any new things popping up, like pride.
5. Draw closer to Jesus every day. Fall in love with Him all over again!
6. Turn it all over to Him and let Him handle the things you need to unpack.

He can handle whatever you need to unpack, even if it is heavy things like drugs, alcohol, pornography, or breaking any of the ten commandments. Pray now and ask God to help you let them go, in the name of Jesus, our Savoir.

UNPACKING BITTERNESS AND UNFORGIVENESS

These will keep you from being effective, in your work, for God. Bitterness and unforgiveness go hand in hand and will stop you in your tracks, preventing you from going on, like banging your head against a brick wall, it isn't moving.

Ephesians 4:31 NIV: *"Get rid of all bitterness, rage and anger, brawling and slander, along with every form of malice. Be kind and compassionate to one another, forgiving each other, just as in Christ, God forgave you."*

Hebrews 12:15 NIV: *"See to it that no one misses the Grace of God and that no bitter root grows up to cause trouble and defile many."*

Bitterness and unforgiveness will keep you from your assigned mission. If you are harboring either one against someone, taking up permanent residence, in your every day existence, you must deal with it head on. It will ruin your life and the lives of those around you. You will never completely heal and be able to go on, unless you let go, of your bitterness and unforgiveness. Pray, with all sincerity, that God will help you let go. Give it all to Him. If you are dealing with this, perhaps you would benefit from a support group that can help you deal with those feelings. One support group that deals specifically with grief and anger due to the death of a loved one,(anyone that was close enough to you that you now have a huge void in your life without them) is *Grief Share* (Grief Share.org). By encouraging others and helping them through this dreadful time, you yourself will heal and you add to your own **spiritual suitcase**. Grief is a painstaking process. Recovery will not happen overnight. But, you will get to the point where you can go on. It will never be the same. You will have a new normal.

NOTES

— CHAPTER FOUR —

The Reoccurring Dream

Several weeks before my husband passed, the Lord Jesus gave me a reoccurring dream and a different way of looking at this impending event; one no one was looking forward to, but knew we could not stop from coming. I wanted to put on the brakes and yell 'STOP'! But, I couldn't do that. It was, as it had always been, in God's hands, not mine. I wanted to wave a magic wand and change all of the present circumstances. I wanted my husband to be well and for us to just enjoy being together again. I had to accept the fact, that I wasn't in control and that was very hard for me. But, I was giving up control, willingly, to Almighty God and there are no better hands to be in.

I want to share the reoccurring dream the Lord kept giving me and I struggled to see the deeper meaning, other than what I saw, on the surface.

Imagine, if you will, a couple, in their late fifties, walking up a set of wide, cream colored, cement steps, from the underground parking garage. There are five steps and he struggles to get up each one, leaning heavily on his bronze colored cane. There is one overhead light, illuminating the stairs. At the top, they turn left, the only way to go. The railroad station is narrow and poorly lit. There are cold metal benches and chairs on either side. Some have backs and some do not. There is no one to answer a question, should they have one. There is what appears to be an office, but the window is closed. The station is dimly lit, yet, a few sparse magazines lay, on the small metal tables attached to the chairs. It is winter and so cold that they can see their breath. They are bundled up with heavy coats, hats, gloves and boots. It is very cold.

Another passenger is an older lady, who for some reason they know is Hungarian. She is wearing a thin scarf over her head, instead of a hat. She is stooped over, squinting to read a book, with her trusty cane at her side.

Another passenger is a tall, slender man, also, much older than the couple. He has on only a thin jacket, much like a windbreaker, and is standing. He is very nervous and apprehensive, as to what is about to take place. He tries to pretend he isn't cold or scared.

Above their heads, against the right wall, is a line of small windows where they can see the railroad tracks. Even though it is late at night, they can see the tracks, because of large lights radianting down, on them from either side.

All three, of the passengers, carry one single suitcase. The suitcases are as different as the people who carry them. They are all old and tattered, but still durable. However, they differ in their heaviness. The elderly lady's is heavy and bulging. The husband's is heavy and difficult to carry, so his wife carries it for him. The wife is not a passenger. She is only there to see her loving husband off, on his long journey. But, the other man's suitcase is very light.

No sooner does the husband sit down and start to read a worn magazine, from 1947, then the train arrives.

They walk slowly up the stairs, at the other end of the building, and onto the platform. The husband and wife go first, then, the Hungarian lady, but the man, in the thin jacket is reluctant and follows them at a slight distance.

The train doors open and two men in black suits, white shirts and ties, step down and help the elderly lady on board. The couple say a tearful goodbye and he boards the train, with the men's help.

His cane falls to the platform and his wife retrieves it. The other man does not get on board. He, nervously, looks down the tracks, for the next train.

The conductor yells, "All aboard!"

The wife takes a step forward, but the men hold up their hands, with a smile, to say, 'stop'. She expects the train to take off further down the tracks, to pick up more passengers, but it doesn't. As she stands watching, the train goes straight up, where Heaven opens and countless people, some in suits, greet the new arrivals. Their smiles light up the sky, as if it were daylight. For an instant, she gets a glimpse of Heaven, longing to go with her husband, but knowing it isn't her time. She puts her hand above her eyes to shade the brightness of the light. Then, the dream ends with the other man still waiting on his train.

Some of this dream was logical to me. The couple was my husband and I. The suitcases they were carrying, held their spiritual wealth. The other man was wearing a thin jacket and unprepared for the cold weather. The Lord showed me this man was also, unprepared to die and to go on to his final destination. He hadn't expected to make this journey now. How often do people put off vitally important decisions that they should make, until it is to late? Then, the decision will be made for them and they are no longer in charge of the choice. It is in God's hands, now.

The Lord showed me that the other two passengers were prepared and ready, even anxious, to go and leave the aches and pains, of this world behind. No more sorrow. No more arthritis, that kept the elderly lady from knitting and doing so many things, like playing with her grandchildren. No more osteoporosis that caused her to stoop, as she sat or walked. No more need for her trusty cane to lean on. No more squinting to read. My husband thought no more Cancer. No more pain. No more suffering. No more waiting for the end.

What are you packing in your *spiritual suitcase*?

FOLLOW UP:

The slender, elderly man, in the thin jacket sees the black train coming down the tracks and smiles, taking a deep breath to calm himself down. He is petrified, but doesn't want anyone else to see. After all he had been a strong, self made man all of his life. He didn't need anyone, but himself. That wasn't about to change now. He didn't need this Jesus or anything else to help him make this final journey.

The black train stops and he gets on. It is pitch black and with much difficulty, he finds a seat. The train takes off, zooming into the night.

NOTES

— CHAPTER FIVE —

The Black Train

As I prayed constantly, over the next few weeks, the Lord Jesus continued to reveal secrets of the unknown world to me.

This last illustration was given to me months after my husband's death. But, this time the interpretation is up to you. You will need to pray that Jesus will make it real for you, as the saying goes 'upfront and personal.'

There are two long trains coming down the track, one is black and one is white. Have you got your ticket ready? Which one are you going to be riding on?

The long black train proceeds onto the dark track. The man waiting, boards the black train and with much difficulty finds a seat. It is pitch black. There are no stars in the sky, no moon or sun to guide his way, only total darkness all around him. He can't even see the person sitting right next to him. He is very afraid. Yet, he can't move from his seat, to escape.

"Why, did I get on board this train?" He tries to shout aloud,

"Stop! I am on the wrong train! Stop, so I can get off!" But, no sound emerges from his now dry mouth. The conductor and other personnel walk up and down the aisles, but he can't utter a word to speak to them. Now, it is too late. The train has left the station and as he looks outside, he can see the lights of the train station, fade away until they become smaller and smaller and eventually disappear all together.

When he had departed, there were many others, all clothed in white robes waiting for their train to arrive. There had been to many to count. They were all carrying a suitcase, not unlike the ones we all carried. Some seemed to struggle with the heaviness of their cases. Some even had two or more suitcases. They all smiled and were jubilant, as they rambled on and on, about their new home waiting for them at the end of the ride.

Why, was his experience so different? He grows more and more fearful until finally, total panic sets in. His heartbeat races rapidly. He screams at the top of his lungs. But, still no sound can be heard.

"Wait!" He yells, "There is a bright light ahead! It must be going to be alright!"

Then, realization comes over him.

"No!" He cries out, "It is my Day of Judgment! I have lived a sinful life. God forgive me!" **But, it is to late.**

Meanwhile, the white train has arrived and the white robed people start to board. In what seems like an instant, they are all seated and anxiously await their departure. They chatter among themselves, laughing and smiling much like excited children on Christmas morning. The bright sun, shines into every corner, of the car, almost blinding each passenger. As the train starts up, a unanimous cheer of joy goes up to Heaven. Everyone begins to sing a song of praise to the Lord Jesus!

Which train, are **you** destined to ride on? Don't you want to change and get on board the white train?

Revelation 20:11-12 & 15 KJV: *"And I saw a great white throne, and Him that sat on it, from whose face the earth and the Heaven fled away; and there was found no place for them. And I saw the dead, small and great, stand before God; and the books were opened: another book was opened, which is*

the book of life. --- And whosoever was not found written in the book of life was cast into the lake of fire." (The lake of fire means Hell)

The man, in the thin jacket, did not have the right ticket for the white train. Do you?

NOTES

— CHAPTER SIX —

The Last Interpretation

Here is the interpretation of the reoccurring dream. No doubt there are others, but this is what was revealed to us, while we prayed in the Spirit. Just as everyone's **spiritual suitcase** is different, so will the interpretation be for each person.

The wide steps: The road, of the world is wide, as we go through life, but the road to the Lord is narrow. We quoted Matthew 7:13-14 earlier. *"Enter through the narrow gate. "*

The underground garage: When we accept Jesus, we come up out of our depths of sin and into our new lives with Him.

   II Corinthians 5:17 NIV: *"Therefore, if anyone is in Christ, he is a new creation; the old has gone, the new has come!"*

Five steps: This represents the five stages, in his life. Jesus has brought him through, even when the husband wasn't aware of it.

1. Infancy
2. Childhood
3. Married
4. Parenting
5. Elderly

Struggles up the stairs: He has had a rough life with many hardships. He didn't want to make this trip. Sometimes, we struggle, in the Christian life.

Ephesians 6:12 KJV: *"For we wrestle not against flesh and blood, but against principalities---against spiritual wickedness in high places."*

The one overhead light: It is Jesus, who is lighting the way.

John 8:12 NIV: *"I am the light of the world. Whoever follows me will never walk in darkness, but will have the light of life."*

The railroad station is dimly lit: As we go through life, the right path may not be well lit and obvious. That is why we must stay in the word and pray daily for God's guidance.

John 14:6 NIV: *"I am the way and the truth and the life. No one comes to the Father except through me."*

The railroad station: Stands for the focal point where everyone, who is about to die, eventually comes. A final gathering place for the dying.

Hebrews 9:27 KJV: *"And as it is appointed unto men once to die, but after this the judgment."*

The cold metal benches: This represents the times the word falls on cold, hard unreceptive ground and is not accepted by those we are witnessing to. Matthew 13:3-9 is the parable of the sower. It pertains very well here. Some were close to accepting Him and others just ignored you. Some will accept the message, some will not. Don't give up! Keep searching for that fertile ground. It's not up to us, it is up to God. He, alone is responsible for the final results.

Are you in the game or are you on the sidelines?

On either side: You have to choose which side you want to be on.

Joshua 24:15 KJV: *"choose you this day whom ye will serve; --but as for me and my house, we will serve the Lord."*

Backs or not: When you are sitting on a cold bench, with no back, you can't relax. You are always ready to jump up, like to do more work for the Lord. If you have a soft chair with a back, symbolically speaking, you can relax and not get as much done for the Kingdom. You can get comfortable in your sin and become immune to the probing of the Holy Spirit.

No one to answer a question: Do you have enough knowledge of the Word of God to answer the questions people will ask you about Jesus?

I Peter 3:15 NIV: *"But in your hearts set apart Christ as Lord. Always be prepared to give an answer to everyone who asks you to give the reason for the hope that you have."*

The office is closed: The time to accept the Lord is limited. There will come a time, when it will be too late. Hebrews 9:27 and Matthew 25:1-13, (the parable of the ten virgins), both give the same idea, the time, to respond is limited.

II Corinthians 6:2b KJV: *"behold, now is the accepted time; behold, now is the day of salvation."*

Sparse magazines: Represents the harvest waiting for workers.

Matthew 9:37 NIV: *"The harvest is plentiful but the workers are few."*

Small tables attached to the chairs: The chairs are stronger and sturdier, because they are attached to the tables. So, we are stronger and sturdier when we are attached to other Christians. We need to join a local church and help support the other Christians on this same road, holding them up when they stumble and visa versa. Encouraging them, praying for them, and helping them, however, you can.

Hebrews 10:25 KJV: *"Not forsaking the assembling of ourselves together--"*

Very cold, hats, coats and gloves: It is very cold in the world. We are fighting an uphill battle. The hats, coats and gloves represents our protection through the power and blood of the Lord Jesus. The world is comfortable, in their sin and doesn't want to hear that they are sinners, and not on their way to Heaven. They don't want us to tell them they are accountable to God or that there is a judgment coming. (Matthew 12: 36) The world tries to cover their sins, in ways other, than Jesus. How do people try to cover their sins and get to Heaven? Perhaps, they carry a huge Bible, or give lots of money to the church or missions. They try to be good and work themselves to Heaven. This will not work. ONLY by accepting the sacrifice of Jesus, on the cross, can we get to Heaven.

The hats, coats and gloves represent that we are **all** covered in the blood of Jesus, and have His absolution for our sins, **if** we have accepted Him as our Savior.

John 14:6 B NIV: *"No one comes to the Father except through me."*

Ephesians 2:8-9 KJV: *"For by grace are ye saved through faith; and that not of yourselves: it is the gift of God.: Not of works, lest any man should boost."*

Hungarian: Faith is not just for Americans, but for everyone, no matter what race, creed or religion. Everyone needs Jesus to get into Heaven.

Mark 16:15 KJV: *"Go ye into all the world, and preach the gospel to every creature."*

We need to take this seriously and not just let it be passing words, like water off of a duck's back. We are **ALL** called to be missionaries, no matter where we are.

The thin scarf:. The scarf represents her worldly possessions. The woman, who is Jewish, is spiritually ready, but is still holding on to a family member (I saw it to be her granddaughter who was about to get married and graduate from college) or something in life that she is having trouble letting go of, such as her ministry.

Stooped over: This could mean that she has kept a secret for a long time, an unconfessed sin, not necessarily her own, but that of a young woman she had counseled. She is a warm and compassionate woman. Her mission in life was to bring other Jews to the Lord. She has carried a heavy burden, for the Lord over the years. She has been a confidant for many and is holding many deep, dark secrets. I do not understand this interpretation, but this was shown to me very clearly.

   Matthew 11:28 KJV: *"Come unto me, all ye that labour and are heavy laden, and I will give you rest."*

Squinting eyes: She is struggling to stay focused, because her time is short. Open your eyes and see His fullness in your life. Don't wait until you have to squint to see Him, until it is to late for you to share your faith.

Cane: She is leaning heavily, on the Lord and keeps Him close at hand, at all times. The cane represents an extension of herself through the ministries that she had in life. In the case of the couple, the wife will now be taking over the ministry they had run together.

Man in thin jacket: He is not a Christian and, therefore, not ready to meet God. Are you?

Above their heads are the tracks: You have to look up to find the right way. Sometimes, as we are going through life, Jesus shows Himself to us in some small ways, that encourages us and helps us through a difficult time. The tracks represents the one and only way, Jesus.

The small line of windows: They could see the light coming through the small line of windows which means Jesus giving us a glimpse of Himself, who is the light.

John 9:5 NIV: *"I am the light of the world."*

John 12:46 NIV: *"I have come into the world as a light, so that no one who believes in me should stay in darkness."*

Suitcases: We all have a suitcase, rather we are Christians or not. We must **choose** to fill our suitcase with our spiritual wealth. First, by accepting Jesus. So, since Jesus MUST be the first thing we put, in our suitcases, the unsaved person's suitcase is empty. (Saved is a Christian word meaning you have accepted the Lord Jesus as your Savior for the forgiveness of your sins.) The man in the thin jacket's suitcase was empty.

1947: People have been going through this same railroad station for all time. Also, in 1947 the Jewish people began returning to Israel. This began a new wave of wars between Israel and the other Arab countries.

Matthew 24: 6 NIV: *"You will hear of wars and rumors of wars."*

This represents that Armageddon will take place just south of Jerusalem, in a location such as the valley of Jehoshaphat, the hill of Megiddo and the **valley of the passengers**. We are using the Wikipedia encyclopedia web site and I am quoting Dr. Pentecost.

The train arrives: We don't know when our time will come, so you need to always be ready. The train always arrives before you expect it.

They walk slowly up the stairs at the other end of the building: Even at the end of this long journey, they still struggle to get through the last endeavor of life. The couple knows it is inevitable, and unavoidable. They wish this wasn't the end, wishing there was some other way, so that they could be together just a little longer. Jesus knew He **had** to die. He knew there was no other way to pay for the sins of the world. He knew what was about to happen and wished there was some other way, yet knowing there was not.

Luke 22:42 KJV: *"Nevertheless not my will, but thine, be done."*

Platform: You have to be at the right place, at the right time if you want to catch the train or lead others to Christ. Always be alert, looking for opportunities to bring others into a loving, saving relationship, with the Lord Jesus. Advance the packing of your *spiritual suitcase,* by using every chance you get to tell others about Jesus.

Suits: They are wearing the full armor of God, Ephesians 6:13-17.

NOTES

— CHAPTER SEVEN —

Packing Your Memories

The next important item to pack, in your suitcase is your memories, every single one of them good or bad. Do you remember running through the wooded area behind your house and playing for hours in never ending fun? Pretending thousands of different things? Pretending you and your friends were pirates and an old log was your ship? Or if you are a girl that you were a princess high in a castle as you sat on a low branch of a strong tree? Do you remember eating meals, at your parents house when you were a child? Do you remember conversations with your brothers and sisters and the fights or arguments? How about your first football game rather you were playing or watching from the cold seats on the side lines? Your high school coach? Your first love? Your first kiss? Your wedding where your mother never stopped crying and your father tried to hold back his tears, unsuccessfully? Your disappointments, like not making the cheerleading squad or the football team? Do you remember, in bright living color, your loving wife and children, your friends and family and even your dog, Buddy? How about those times of sheer terror? And that time you rode that roller coaster, then regretted it?

Pack all your memories, in your suitcase, in the very back, in the large pouch. That pouch is removable, so you can unpack any memories you don't want to remember. The death of a loved one or serious injury to you or a close family member might be something you'd want to remove. You need to pack all of your memories carefully.

YOUR WHOLE LIFE YOU ARE PACKING YOUR SPIRITUAL SUITCASE WITH MEMORIES.

Do you remember the numerous church services you attended, some good, some not so good? Do you remember playing the tambourine for all to hear and singing hymns? Do you remember when we saw the television evangelist and how he laid hands on you and prayed for your recovery? How about reading the Bible late at night when you couldn't sleep, which was often? Or early in the morning when everyone else was still sleeping?

Or the verses that leapt out of those Holy pages, to help you through the rough times? How many times did you have no idea which way to turn and a verse would show you that God's hand is always on you?

God has a reason for each and every thing that happens to you. When do you grow in the Lord and add the most to your *spiritual suitcase,* during good times or bad, on the mountain top or in the valley? You always grow more in the valleys. So, I would not choose to remove any of the memories, because those bad times are when I held on the tightest to the Lord Jesus.

Those are the times that will solidify your faith in the Lord. Those valleys are when you draw, on the strong foundation you have established. He will bring to your memory the many verses you have heard, read or memorized, to strengthen you and give you the courage to go on. Amen! Thank you, Jesus!

The most important memories, to remember is your life with the Lord Jesus. Do you remember when you first trusted Him for your eternal salvation? Do you remember leading people to the Lord at the flea market or wherever you went? Do you remember carrying the Spanish Bibles for people to take? That is a personal memory, but you can correlate to your own life. Did you pass out tracts? Did you stand, on the street and tell others about the Lord? You need to make your own memories concerning the Lord Jesus. What is comfortable for one person, might not be for another. But, wherever you are, you need to always be aware that there are people, all around you that need to be saved and hand their eternal destination over to the Lord. You need to find your niche. What works for you? I add a line or two when I am in a chat room for people over, well let's just say older adults. Ok, over 50! There, I've said it.

Maybe, you are on the bus or subway, or in the car with a willful teenager. Just a comment, can get them thinking about the Lord. Maybe, you have read a good book, by a number of Christian authors. You could pass it on to an unsaved friend with a comment like this.

"I know we may not believe exactly the same, but I just finished reading this great book! It really gave me a lot to think about. I think you would enjoy it too."

Pray and ask God what you can do to further the Kingdom of God.

On another thought, what have you taken <u>out</u> of your ***spiritual suitcase*** that you shouldn't have? What work did you use to do for the Lord that you are not doing now? Have you taken yourself out of the Lord's Army? Have you issued your own discharge papers? Or, are you adding to your ***spiritual suitcase*** every day? Have you removed the detachable pouch, from your suitcase, therefore, not having it available to add more memories, in the future? Have you slipped back into sin? Have you stopped going to church on Wednesday nights, because your favorite show is on television?

MAKE YOUR OWN MEMORIES FOR JESUS TODAY!

Proverbs 10:7 KJV: *"The memory of the just is blessed--"*

NOTES

— CHAPTER EIGHT —

Packing The Work You've Done 'In The Name Of Jesus'

Another very important item to pack is the work you have done *'in the Name of Jesus.'* You want to pack this in the very front of your suitcase. Only that which is done with the right motives will last.

I Corinthians 3:13 NIV: "*his work will be shown for what it is -- fire will test the quality of each man's work.*"

Are you endeavoring to seek out people to tell about Jesus and His love? How many people have you led to the Lord? Have you lost track? Are they to numerous to count? Great! That is more souls that will be in Heaven, and not in Hell, for eternity. Those have been added to your *spiritual suitcase*.

Did you ever consider the eternal value of your every action, thought or word? We are accountable, to the Lord, for every moment of our lives. How did you use your time? Every space spent doing selfish or unproductive things is wasted time. That spot, in your *spiritual suitcase*, will be empty, instead of overflowing to the point that you have to sit on it, to get it closed. How many more people might have been saved or helped through a crisis in their lives, if only you had taken the time to speak up? You will be missing out on the joy helping others can bring, if you are a self-centered person and not a people centered person. Which are you?

Colossians 3:2 KJV: *"Set your affection on things above, not on things on the earth."*

Matthew 6:33 KJV: *"But seek ye first the kingdom of God, and his righteousness; and all these things shall be added unto you."*

UNPACKING FEAR

But, maybe you have never led anyone to the Lord. No time like the present to do so! Your *spiritual suitcase* is still open. Many churches offer classes to teach you how to evangelize. Don't be afraid! The Lord will be right there with you. He will guide you on what to do and say. Just ask Him. Be strong.

Joshua 1:9 NIV: *"Have I not commanded you? Be strong and courageous. Do not be terrified; do not be discouraged, for the Lord your God will be with you wherever you go."*

II Timothy 1:7 KJV: *"For God hath not given us the spirit of fear; but of power, and of love, and of a sound mind."*

Hebrews 13:5 KJV: *"I will never leave thee, nor forsake thee."*

PACKING WINNING SOULS FOR JESUS

Never do you add more to your *spiritual suitcase*, then when you are winning souls for the Lord. In order to do that, you must start by praising Him, daily/constantly for His many blessings in your life. As soon as you get up in the morning, start purposely, finding things to thank and praise Him for. "Thank you, that I have a home. Thank you, that I have Your Word to read." We must confess our sins, daily, and ask for His forgiveness. You need to have a clean heart. Read the Word and pray daily. Worship Jesus daily, with all of your heart and soul.

Do you have a passion for the lost? If not, pray and ask the Lord to give this to you. **If** we do not tell them, how will they know? Don't leave this for someone else to do. What if they don't do it? Is Heaven and Hell and the fact that people will be judged some day, a reality to you ? We **must** tell them!

Romans 10:14-15 KJV: *"How shall they hear without a preacher?--- How beautiful are the feet of them that preach the tidings of good things!"* Jesus commands us all:

Matthew 28:19 NIV: *"Therefore go and make disciples of all nations, baptizing them in the name of the Father and of the Son and of the Holy Spirit--And surely I am with you always, to the very end of the age."*

This is not an option. It is a command**.** Go above and beyond, in your work for God. Don't be compliant or nonchalant. What might happen, if you gave it your all? I don't want to be just going through the motions. Do you? You need to step out, step up to the plate and hit a home run for the Lord's team! You need to challenge yourself to go further than ever before. If not now, when? Reach for the stars for the Lord! You can do **anything,** in Jesus' name and power. If it has never been done, then that mission field is white and ready for the harvest.

John 4:35-36 NIV: *"I tell you, open your eyes and look at the fields! They are ripe for harvest. Even now the reaper draws his wages, even now he harvests the crop for eternal life, so that the sower and the reaper may be glad together."*

We had never heard of anyone having a ministry at the flea market, but that is what God told us to do, so we did and we saw people saved and touched by God.

Philippians 4:13 KJV: *"I can do all things through Christ which strengtheneth me."*

II Thessalonians 3:3 NIV: *"But the Lord is faithful, and He will strengthen and protect you from the evil one."*

Isaiah 41:10 NIV: *"So do not fear, for I am with you; do not be dismayed, for I am your God. --- I will uphold you with my righteous right hand."*

Pastor Greg Laurie said, when he had only been saved for two weeks, he read the *'Four Spiritual Laws'* tract to a woman and even though he did it, very poorly, she patiently listened. Then, to his total shock, she prayed to accept the Lord Jesus! He had basically no training. God is in charge, of the situation and He is responsible for the results, not us. We must leave it in His hands.

PACKING MEMORIZING THE WORD OF GOD

Hebrews 4:12 KJV: *"For the Word of God is quick, and powerful, and sharper than any two-edged sword."*

Hebrews 4:12 NIV: *"For the word of God is living and active. Sharper than any double-edged sword."*

If you are not meticulously, into the Word, how can you answer the questions people might have, when you go to tell them about Jesus? We must memorize the Word of God.

Psalm 119:11 NIV: says, *"I have hidden your Word in my heart that I might not sin against you."*

If you are witnessing, it will not give the person any confidence, if you can't quote or at least find the verses in the Bible. Spend time daily with the Word of God. How many verses can you quote, chapter and verse? Do you search for answers, in the Holy Scriptures? If not, where **do you** draw your strength from? Do you dive into the word seeking, tirelessly, learning and memorizing, as Pastor Rogers used to say, *"The golden nuggets"* in the Bible? Is there a specific time, each day when you get together, with the Lord Jesus and on your face, seeking His will for your life, not just for that day, but for your life in general? Are you in church every week, studying the Word and fellowshipping with fellow believers?

I am reading a great devotional book, *'Twelve Months of Sundays'* by Miss Nan. She has this, to add on the subject of the devil. ***"How should we resist him? We must use, the Sword of*** *the Spirit. To use it, we have to know it. Memorize scripture."* (The Sword of the Spirit is the Bible.)

Take up your Sword and use it against the devil! He doesn't want you to lead any more people to the Lord. He <u>will</u> fight you tooth and nail. He <u>will</u> come against you. **BUT JESUS IS STONGER THAN THE DEVIL!**

I John 4:4 NIV: *" The one who is in you is greater than the one who is in the world."*

One weapon we have is the Word of God. We can only use what we have in our arsenal. Jesus used the Word of God, when He was tempted in the desert.

Matthew 4:4 KJV: *"It is written, Man shall not live by bread alone, but by every word that proceeded out of the mouth of God."*

PACKING PRAYER AS A WEAPON

How often do you pray? Not 'thank you Jesus for this food amen' type prayer, but diligently seeking God's face, type prayer. This will dramatically influence your effectiveness to the work of the Lord. **You can not be a soul winner and successfully work for Jesus, if you are not a prayer warrior**.

II Chronicles 7:14 NIV: *"if my people, who are called by my name, will humble themselves and pray and seek my face and turn from their wicked ways, then will I hear from Heaven and will forgive their sin and heal their land."*

Philippians 4:6 NIV: *"Do not be anxious about anything, but in everything, by prayer and petition, with thanksgiving, present your requests to God."*

Matthew 7:7 NIV: *"Ask and it will be given to you; seek and you will find; knock and the door will be opened to you."* How do you ask? Only through prayer can we communicate with God, through Jesus, His only Son.

I Thessalonians 5:17 KJV: *"Pray without ceasing."*

When Jesus was in the Garden of Gethsemane, He prayed. When, He was on the cross, He prayed. So, should we. Add to your ***spiritual suitcase,*** by praying passionately every day. Pray with others who need help. Pray that the Lord will show you His way for your life. PRAY!

PACKING TRUST IN JESUS AS YOUR GUIDE

I John 4:4 KJV: *"Greater is He that is in you, than he that is in the world."* The Lord will strengthen you.

II Timothy 1:12 NIV: *"---Yet I am not ashamed, because I know whom I have believed, and am convinced that He is able to guard what I have entrusted to Him for that day."* He is guarding whatever you pack in your ***spiritual suitcase***!

Romans 8:37-39 KJV: *"In all these things we are more than conquerors through Him that loved us. For I am persuaded, that neither death, nor life, nor angels, nor principalities, nor powers, nor things present, nor things to come--- shall be able to separate us from the love of God, which is in Christ Jesus our Lord."*

Romans 8:31 KJV: *"If God be for us, who can be against us?"*

What more could we possibly need?

Mark 10:27: also in the KJV reminds us *"With men it is impossible, but not with God: for with God all things are possible."*

As you go about trying to tell others, about Jesus and His eternal Salvation, remember **anything** is possible. The lost souls need to know the only way to have their sins forgiven; the only way to get their one way ticket to Heaven, when they die, is through faith in Jesus Christ. TELL THEM!

Psalm 37:28-29 & 31 NIV: *"For the Lord loves the just and will not forsake His faithful ones. They will be protected* *forever, but the offspring of the wicked will be cut off; the righteous will inherit the land and dwell in it forever. The law of his God is in his heart; his feet do not slip.*" He is watching over us.

PACKING THE CONCEPT OF SOWING AND REAPING

We will reap what we sow. If you sow evil and selfishness, that is what you will reap. You can't plant an apple tree and expect to get cherries.

Galatians 6:7-10 NIV: *"Do not be deceived: God can not be mocked. A man reaps what he sows. The one who sows to please his sinful nature, from that nature will reap destruction; the one who sows to please the Spirit, from the Spirit will reap eternal life. Let us not become weary in doing good, for at the proper time we will reap a harvest if we do not give up. Therefore, as we have opportunity, let us do good to all people.*"

You can be ineffective to the work of the Kingdom, if you are focusing on the things of this world and yourself and not on Jesus.

Mark 4:19 NIV: *"but the worries of this life, the deceitfulness of wealth and the desires for other things come in and choke the word, making it unfruitful."*

PACKING SERVING OTHERS / UNPACKING SELFISHNESS

Do you feel down and depressed? Start praising the Lord! Go help someone less fortunate. Begin to, literally, count your many blessings. Get on your knees and pray for other people, crying out to God on their behalf. Pray for the people you know who have real needs, and who are desperate for God and His help with certain situations., the widow, who has lost her job or maybe a fatherless child. Men, if there is a boy, who has no father figure in his life take him with you to a ballgame. It would be a priceless time for him and at the same time, you would be adding to your *spiritual suitcase*. Admit it! You would enjoy that time, too.

Philippians 2:3-5 NIV: *"Do nothing out of selfish ambition or vain conceit, but in humility consider others better than yourselves. Each of you should look not only to your own interests, but also to the interests of others. Your attitude should be the same as that of Christ Jesus."*

Have you done something to help another person out of a tight spot, 'in the Name of Jesus'? Maybe, a single mother was a little short on grocery money. You could have helped her without putting a strain on your own budget. Did you? Did you, then tell her about Jesus? Maybe, you took time to help an elderly man, to the car, with his purchases, at the big discount store. It only took a few minutes, but it meant so much to him. As an example, you are behind a woman, in the grocery store checkout line, who is counting change to buy cereal and milk for her children. You quietly step forward and swipe your card and give her the change back. You just added to your *spiritual suitcase*. But, if you make a big deal and say loudly, " Here little lady, let me help you with that," looking around to make sure everyone hears, then you have gotten your reward. This won't be added to your *spiritual suitcase*.

Matthew 6:1 & 2 NKJV: *"Take heed that you do not do your charitable deeds before men, to be seen by them. Otherwise you have no reward from your Father in Heaven. Therefore, when you do a charitable deed, do not sound a trumpet before you as the hypocrites do in the synagogues and in the streets, that they may have glory from men. Assuredly, I say to you, they have their reward."*

Did you teach the Sunday School class no one else wanted, or maybe you sang in the choir where many were blessed? NOT for your glory, but His, so that our Lord Jesus would be honored and raised up? Did you work at the homeless shelter or clean up after a revival meeting or answer the phones at your church?

These are all part of your *spiritual suitcase*. As long as you are doing the job, unto the Lord and not for your own selfish gains, that will have a spot in your *spiritual suitcase*. If you love Him, you will be working to bring others to Him .

I want to repeat myself. If you have times, in your life, when you blow off an opportunity, to help someone, or to speak to them about the Lord Jesus t**hat space in your suitcase will be empty**. You can not bring back a missed opportunity!

PACKING MERCY

Mercy and forgiveness, also go hand in hand. **If you do not show mercy, you will not be shown mercy**. It is very important that you have compassion and help those in need, "in the Name of Jesus." By showing mercy and forgiveness to others, people will see Jesus, in your life.

James 2:13 NKJV: *"For judgment is without mercy to the one who has shown no mercy. Mercy triumphs over judgment."*

Titus 3:5 NIV: *"He saved us, not because of righteous things we had done, but because of His mercy."*

I Peter 1:3 NIV: *"Praise be to the God and Father of our Lord Jesus Christ! In His great mercy he has given us new birth into a living hope through the resurrection of Jesus Christ from the dead."*

PACKING LOVE FOR EACH OTHER

Matthew 22:37-39 NIV: *"Love the Lord your God with all your heart and with all your soul and with all your mind. This is the first and greatest commandment. And the second is like it: Love your neighbor as yourself."*

John 13:34-35 KJV: *"A new commandment I give unto you, That ye love one another; as I have loved you, that ye also* *love one another. By this shall all men know that ye are my disciples, if ye have love one to another."*

Matthew 5:44-45 NIV: tells us to *"Love your enemies and pray for those who persecute you,--He causes his sun to rise on the evil and the good, and sends rain on the righteous and the unrighteous."*

Psalm 118:1 NIV: "Give thanks to the Lord, for he is good; his love endures forever."

UNPACKING APATHY AND LAZINESS FOR THE LORD

To many Christians are sitting in their comfortable chairs, doing **nothing** for the Lord. Imagine, a person, in a recliner, with the foot rest up, a cool drink, in one hand and the remote in the other. Many Christians have become lazy for the Lord. They go to church, but that is as far as it goes. They would never witness! They would never pass out a gospel tract or invite a stranger or a even a friend to a church service or a special event. They are keeping their faith to themselves. They do not want to draw attention to themselves and are embarrassed to do so. What if Jesus had said that? He was humiliated and embarrassed, for our sake. He died the death of a criminal, for our sake. Yet, we don't want to **risk** drawing attention to ourselves? He gave His all and paid a debt He didn't owe, for our sake.

Romans 1:16 KJV: *"For I am not ashamed of the gospel of Christ: for it is the power of God unto salvation to every one that believeth."*

Matthew 5:14 &16 KJV: *"Ye are the light of the world.--- Let your light so shine before men, that they may see your good works, and glorify your Father which is in Heaven."*

Proverbs 18:9 NIV: *"One who is slack in his work is brother to one who destroys."* Don't be lazy in your work for the Lord. Time is short.

AN APATHETIC CHRISTIAN HAS NO POWER!
APATHY WILL KILL THE EFFECTIVENESS OF THE CHURCH!

This is exactly what the devil wants! If he can steal your power through apathy, there will be no new converts, because he has already stolen your desire to work for the Lord. You will limit your usefulness to the Kingdom, if that happens. You may be going to Heaven, but are you taking anyone with you?

Are you on the Lord's side or not? Can He count on you to come through for Him? Are you hurting the ministry by being a bad example, by your laziness and apathetic ways, in your work for the Lord?

Mark 9:40 NIV: *"for whoever is not against us is for us."*

Romans 12:11 NIV: *"Never be lacking in zeal, but keep your spiritual fervor, serving the Lord.*

Romans 12:11 NKJV: *"…not lagging in diligence, fervent in Spirit, serving the Lord."*

Romans 12:11 The Message: *"Don't burn out; Keep yourselves fueled and aflame. Be alert servants of the Master cheerfully expectant. Don't quit in hard times; pray all the harder."*

And the New Living Translation says:

Romans 12:11 *"Don't be lazy, but work hard and serve the Lord enthusiastically."*

Romans 13:11 KJV: *"…Knowing the time, that now it is high time to awake out of sleep: for now is our salvation nearer than when we believed."*

The Message says it this way:

"But make sure that you don't get so absorbed and exhausted in taking care of all your day to day obligations that you lose track of the time and doze off, oblivious to God. The night is about over, dawn is about to break. Be up and awake to what God is doing! God is putting the finishing touches on the salvaion work He began when we first believed. We can't afford to waste a minute, must not squander these precious daylight hours in frivolity and indulgence …… Get out of bed and get dressed! Don't loiter and linger, waiting until the very last minute. Dress yourselves in Christ and be up and about."

That really says the points I am trying to make.

PACKING STANDING FIRM

Is there a need for a ministry and no one to lead the way? Take the reigns and run with it! We can do all things through Christ that strengthens us, but we can do **NOTHING** without Him right beside us giving us His power. We are powerless without Him! You wouldn't go into battle without your weapons, your Sword of the Spirit, your shield of faith, your helmet of salvation, your breastplate of righteousness. You are leading with your shield, which protects you from the fiery darts of the devil.

Ephesians 6:16 NIV: *"In addition to all this, take up the shield of faith, with which you can extinguish all the flaming arrows of the evil one."*

Ephesians 6:13-14 NIV: *"Therefore put on the full armor of God, so that when the day of evil comes, you may be able to stand your ground, and after you have done everything, to stand. Stand firm."*

Mark 13:13 NIV: *"All men will hate you because of me, but he who stands firm to the end will be saved."*

DO NOT be afraid! **DO NOT** waiver. Remember,

Hebrews 13:5 KJV: *"I WILL NEVER LEAVE THEE, NOR FORSAKE THEE."* Never, means never!

Isaiah 40:28 & 31 NIV: *"The Lord is the everlasting God---He will not grow tired or weary, ---They will soar on wings like eagles; they will run and not grow weary, they will walk and not be faint."*

II Peter 1:5-8 NIV: *"For this very reason, make every effort to add to your faith, goodness; and to goodness, knowledge, and to knowledge, self-control and to self control, perseverance, and to perseverance, godliness, and to godliness, brotherly kindness and to brotherly kindness, love. For if you possess these qualities in increasing measure, they will keep you from being ineffective and unproductive in your knowledge of our Lord Jesus Christ."*

NOTES

— CHAPTER NINE —

Packing Your Mission Packing Your Spiritual Gifts

The next item to pack is your mission in life. **We all have a mission.** Have you discovered what yours is? Are you accomplishing your mission? Are you praying and asking the Lord to show you exactly what it is, He wants you to do for Him? Or are you just sitting around "hoping" to fall into it? He may not tell you the whole mission all at once, because if He did, most of us couldn't handle it. But, it is i**mperative** that you find out what your mission is.

Your mission and your work, for the Lord are connected. Look at it this way, the work, you do may be one task. For example, helping at the church's clothes closet or helping a person in need. But, your mission is a more long term commitment to that cause. It could be as a minister or as a teacher or serving as a leader for divorce care. Your mission will not be exactly like anyone else's. What are you **passionate** about? Not everyone is called to be a missionary, in a far away land, but, we are **all** called to be missionaries wherever we are.

Proverbs 3:5-6 KJV: *"Trust in the Lord with all thine heart; and lean not unto thine own understanding. In all thy ways*

acknowledge Him, and He shall direct thy paths." He will show you your mission when you pray and ask Him.

PACKING YOUR SPIRITUAL GIFTS

First, you need to know what your spiritual gifts are. Discovering this, will help you to determine and accomplish your mission. What are the spiritual gifts?

I Corinthians 12:1 NIV: *" Now about spiritual gifts, brothers, I do not want you to be ignorant."*

Do you have the gift of teaching? The gift of wisdom? Or maybe healing? The gift of knowledge or helps? Prophecy? The discerning of spirits? Tongues? Or the interpretation of tongues? Or is it administration? You need to be using whatever gifts God has given you to serve Him.

Don't even say you have no gift! We all have a gift given to us, by God, in order to do His will and work here on Earth.

The most important gift of all is love.

I Corinthians 12:31 NIV: *"But eagerly desire the greater gifts."*

The entire chapter of 1Corinthians 13 is about love.

I Corinthians 13:3 NIV: *"If I give all I possess to the poor and surrender my body to the flames, but have not love, I gain nothing."*

I Corinthians 13:8 NIV: *"Love never fails."* Read chapters 12 and 13 to better understand spiritual gifts. Where can you improve in this area of your life? Every time you show genuine love for someone, you add to your own *spiritual suitcase.*

Let's start with a list of the spiritual gifts, so you can see where your gift may lie.

1. Wisdom
2. Knowledge
3. Faith
4. Healing

5. Miracles
6. Prophecy
7. Discerning of spirits
8. Tongues
9. Interpretation of Tongues
10. Administration
11. Helps

The gift of wisdom is the ability to make decisions and give guidance that is according to God's will.

The gift of knowledge is the ability to have an in-depth understanding of a spiritual issue or situation.

The gift of faith is being able to trust God and encourage others to trust God, no matter what the circumstances.

The gift of healing is the miraculous ability to use God's healing power to restore a person who is sick, injured or suffering.

The gift of miracles is being able to perform signs and wonders that give authenticity to God's Word and the Gospel message.

The gift of prophecy is being able to proclaim a message from God.

The gift of discerning spirits is the ability to determine whether or not a message, person or event is truly from God.

The gift of tongues is the ability to speak in a foreign language that you do not have knowledge of, in order to communicate with someone who speaks that language or to communicate with God.

The gift of interpreting tongues is the ability to translate the tongues being spoken and communicate it back to others in your own language.

The gift of administration is being able to keep things organized and in accordance with God's principles.

The gift of helps is always having the desire and ability to help others, to do whatever it takes to get a task accomplished.

If you do not know what your mission is or what your gifts are, pray and ask the Lord to reveal the answer to you. Ask your pastor to pray with you. **This is important**. You need to be heading in the right direction.

Again, where does your passion lie? Is it working with children and watching their little faces light up when you talk about Jesus? Or just talking with elderly people at the nursing home? Or helping the sick? Helping the homeless? Pack your mission in your *spiritual suitcase*. Accomplish your full assignment for God by utilizing all the gifts the Lord has given you. Reach new heights for Jesus. Challenge yourself, today! Do not be at the end of your life wondering, "What if I had---." Fill in the blanks, with, told others about Jesus, or helped that lonely widow or whatever. What could have happened, if you had given your **all** to the cause of Christ, instead of saying, "Whatever, let someone else do it."

Your mission will change as you go through life. For example, parents have a mission to raise their children, in the admiration of the Lord. But, after the children leave home and have lives of their own, the parents are now going to have a different mission to accomplish, or maybe, intensify their work for the Lord. When your children are at home and in school, it would be hard to go on a mission trip. But, when they move out, the parents would be more free to travel. This is how your mission might change. When you are working a regular job, you are limited to the time you can invest. But, when you retire you have all the time you need. Be passionate about your mission for God.

NOTES

— CHAPTER TEN —

Don't Be Judgmental
Unpacking Being Judgmental

One thing that might keep you from being effective in your work, for the Kingdom, is if you are judgmental. I will admit, I struggle in this area.

Matthew 7:1-2 NIV: *"Do not judge, or you too will be judged. For in the same way you judge others, you will be judged, and with the measure you use, it will be measured to you."*

If you think you are better than someone else, read this verse, again.

Romans 3:23 NIV: *"For all have sinned and fall short of the Glory of God."* **Matthew 7:12 NIV:** *"Do to others what you would have them do to you."*

Do you do this? Or do you look at a dirty, ragged person and assume they are a drunk? Or at a woman in an immodest dress and assume she is a prostitute?

James 2:1-4 NIV: *"My brothers, as believers in our glorious Lord Jesus Christ, don't show favoritism. Suppose a man comes into your meeting wearing a gold ring and fine clothes, and a poor man in shabby clothes also comes in. If you show special attention to the man wearing fine clothes and say, "Here's a* *good seat for you," but say to the poor man, "You stand there" or "Sit on the floor by my feet," have you not discriminated among yourselves and become judges with evil thoughts?"*

Matthew 7:4-5 NIV: *"How can you say to your brother, 'Let me take the speck out of your eye,' when all the time there is a plank in your own eye? You hypocrite, first take the plank out of your own eye, and then you will see clearly to remove the speck from your brother's eye.".*

Do you discriminate between wealthy and poor people; people with education and people who can barely read or write? Black from white? God sees us as equals. God is the judge, not us.

James 4:11-12 NIV: *"Brothers, do not slander one another. Anyone who speaks against his brother or judges him speaks against the law and judges it. -- There is only one Lawgiver and Judge, the one who is able to save and destroy. But you---who are you to judge your neighbor?"*

Acts 15:8-9 NIV: *"God, who knows the heart, showed that He accepted them by giving the Holy Spirit to them, just as He did to us. He made no distinction between us and them, for he purified their hearts by faith."*

Romans 10:12-13 NIV: *"For there is no difference between Jew and Gentile--the same Lord is Lord of all and richly blesses all who call on Him, for, everyone who calls on the name of the Lord will be saved."*

Neither should we discriminate between different people. Are you only friends with popular people? But, ignore the ones no one else talks to? They all need Jesus in their lives. Do not judge. Hard isn't it? But, with God's help we can do it. You can't do this without the Lord. But, with Him, all things are possible.

Jeremiah 32:27 NIV: *"I am the Lord, the God of all mankind. Is anything too hard for me?"* No, nothing.

Romans 14:12-13 NIV: *"So then, each of us will give an account of himself to God. Therefore let us stop passing judgment on one another. Instead, make up your mind not to put any stumbling block or obstacle in your brother's way."*

NOTES

CHAPTER ELEVEN

Packing Your Money
Unpacking The Money Idol

Another thing that could keep you from being effective, in the work of the Kingdom, is your money management. How do you handle the resources that the Lord has blessed you with? The Bible says, that at least 10% of your income should go toward the work of the Lord. This is your tithe. I think many people struggle in this area.

Malachi 3: 8-10 NIV: *"Will a man rob God? ---How do we rob you? "In tithes and offerings. You are under a curse--the whole nation--because you are robbing me. Bring the whole tithe into the storehouse, that there may be food in my house. Test me in this," says the Lord Almighty, "and see if I will not throw open the floodgates of heaven and pour out so much blessing that you will not have room enough for it."*

Through your faithfulness, in this area, the Lord will bless you and you will add to your *spiritual suitcase*.

You often hear people say, you can't out give God. I have tested this theory many times, and found it to be true. As a single mother for over 9 years, I had to hold tightly to the hand of Jesus, for our provisions. If you don't trust the Lord to handle the finances you have, why should He give you more? If you keep all of your money for yourself, you have forgotten that it all belongs to the Lord.

Genesis 1:1 NIV: *"In the beginning God created the Heavens and the Earth."*

He made everything and has only loaned it to you for awhile.

Colossians 3:1-3 KJV: *"If ye then be risen with Christ, seek those things which are above, where Christ sitteth on the right hand of God. Set your affection on things above, not on things on the earth. For ye are dead, and your life is hid with Christ in God."*

Numbers 18:29 NIV: *"You must present as the Lord's portion the best and holiest part of everything given to you."*

Are you making money an idol in your life? Jesus often spoke about money. Are you making money your god?

Matthew 6:24 NIV: *"No one can serve two masters. Either he will hate the one and love the other, or he will be devoted to the one and despise the other. You can not serve both God and Money."*

Exodus 20:3-4 KJV: *"Thou shalt have no other gods before me. Thou shalt not make unto thee any graven image, or any likeness of anything that is in Heaven above, or that is in the earth beneath."*

I Timothy 6:10 NIV: *"For the love of money is a root of all kinds of evil. Some people, eager for money, have wandered from the faith and pierced themselves with many griefs."*

Won't you make yourself a promise to do better at this in the coming year? You will not regret it! Remember:

Philippians 4:19 KJV: *"But my God shall supply all your need according to His riches in glory by Christ Jesus."*

God owns the cattle on the hills.

Psalm 50:10-11 NIV: *"for every animal of the forest is mine, and the cattle on a thousand hills. I know every bird in the mountains, and the creatures of the field are mine."*

Proverbs 3:9-10 KJV: *"Honour the Lord with thy substance, and with the first-fruits of all thine increase; So shall thy barns be filled with plenty, and thy presses shall burst out with new wine."*

Luke 6:38 NIV: *"Give, and it will be given to you. A good measure, pressed down, shaken together and running over, will be poured into your lap. For with the measure you use, it will be measured to you."*

NOTES

— CHAPTER TWELVE —

Unpacking Pride

Another thing that can keep you from being effective, in your work for the Kingdom of God, is pride. We all know the story, in the Bible about how Satan aspired to be God and thought he could do that. But, there is only one God.

Isaiah 14:12-15 KJV: *"--O Lucifer, son of the morning! How art thou cut down to the ground,-----For thou hast said in thine heart, I will ascend into Heaven, I will exalt my throne above the stars of God: I will sit also upon the mount of the congregation, in the sides of the north: I will ascend above the heights of the clouds; I will be like the most High. Yet thou shalt be brought down to hell, to the sides of the pit."*

Exodus 20:2-3 NIV: *"I am the Lord your God, who brought you out of Egypt, out of the land of slavery. You shall have no other gods before me."*

On a side note, what has Jesus brought **you** out of? Drugs? Alcohol, pornography, unfaithfulness to God? You and God know what your downfalls have been. You were enslaved to sin, but He brought you to a higher ground and forgave you of all unrighteousness.

Romans 3:10 KJV: *"As it is written, There is none righteous, no, not one."*

What was Satan's downfall? Pride and covetousness.

Job 35:12-13 KJV: *"There they cry, but none giveth answer, because of the pride of evil men. Surely God will not hear vanity, neither will the Almighty regard it."*

Proverbs 8:13 NIV: *"To fear the Lord is to hate evil; I hate pride and arrogance, evil behavior and perverse speech."*

Proverbs 16:18 KJV: *"Pride goeth before destruction, and an haughty spirit before a fall."*

Proverbs 29:23 NIV: *"A man's pride brings him low, but a man of lowly spirit gains honor."*

There are many more throughout the whole Bible, but the point is, that if you are prideful, your work for the Lord will be greatly diminished. Being proud and prideful is a sin. Have your pastor pray with you, if this is an area of concern for you. Don't be prideful, because as you have seen from these verses, it will be your downfall.

Let's talk about Peter. He was fine as long as he had his eyes on Jesus. He looked out and saw Jesus, walking on the water. He was fine when he stepped out of boat. He was fine when he walked on the water to Jesus. But, when he realized that he was doing the impossible, he fell. So it is with pride. When we take our eyes off of Jesus and put the attention on ourselves that is when we fall.

UNPACKING JEALOUSY/ENVY/ANGER

In Genesis 4:4-8, we have the story of what jealousy can do. Cain was jealous that Abel's gift, to God was accepted and his wasn't. He was so angry that he killed his brother. Be happy when others succeed, not jealous or envious of them.

Proverbs 14:30 NLT: *"A peaceful heart leads to a healthy body; jealousy is like cancer in the bones."*

Proverbs 27:4 NLT: *"Anger is cruel, and wrath is like a flood, but jealousy is even more dangerous."*

Acts 5:17 NLT: *"The high priest and his officials, who were Sadducees, were filled with jealousy."*

Philippians 1:15 NIV: *"It is true that some preach Christ out of envy and rivalry, but others out of goodwill."*

Galatians 5:19-20 NIV: *"The acts of the sinful nature are obvious: sexual immorality, impurity and debauchery; idolatry and witchcraft; hatred, discord, jealousy, fits of rage, selfish ambition, dissensions, factions, and envy; drunkenness, orgies, and the like. I warn you, as I did before, that those who live like this will not inherit the Kingdom of God."*

Jealousy is more important than some of us think. Unpack all of these things out of your *spiritual suitcase* today.

NOTES

— CHAPTER THIRTEEN —

Packing Your Testimony Packing Victory

Your testimony **has** to be a good one. Do people **know** you are a Born Again, on your way to Heaven, Christian? Do you witness with your life? Or do you have one foot in the world and the other one with Jesus? Do you put on your "Christian face" when you go to church and act like everyone else, Monday through Saturday?

James 5:12 NIV: *"Above all, my brothers, do not swear- not by Heaven or by earth --Let your "Yes" be yes, and your "No," no, or you will be condemned."*

I want to share my husband's testimony with you, to encourage you and to assure you that anything, yes, I mean anything is possible when the Lord Jesus is with you. This testimony is to the glory of God, not for my glory.

Philippians 4:13 NKJV: *"I can do all things through Christ who strengthens me."*

There comes a time, in every Christian's life, when they need to ask themselves, "Do I <u>really</u> believe Jesus is capable of handling everything in my life, or are these just words?" It became apparent, very quickly, that we really did believe, but that we were about to be greatly tested. Once you have accepted Jesus, the devil can not get your soul, but he can steal your testimony. My husband and I prayed that we would be found worthy.

First, you must determine, through prayer and supplication, if you are in the will of God. If you are unsure, ask your pastor to pray with you. This is very important. If you aren't, that could be the reason you are being tested.

In 2001, my husband, Eddie, and I opened a business at the flea market, mainly selling used clothes. While we worked, we passed out Spanish and English gospel tracts and New Testaments. We always took the time to pray with people and added their names to our prayer list.

I want to make one point very clear. The devil **can not** mess with you, if you are under the blood of Jesus! Jesus is watching out for us and is on our side. Thank God for that point! Psalm 124 tells us how lost we are without God on our side.

In April 2005, we got word that my mother-in-law was very ill and Eddie needed to go to Colombia (South America) and see her, immediately. She was asking for him. When he tried to come back, into the United States, Immigration said his papers weren't in order. He had lived and worked legally, in this country, for 39 years. But, they were questioning everyone since the 9-11 attacks. The devil thought 'I got him now!' **He didn't**. Over the next few months, they called him in, time and time again to question him. In September, they detained him for 6 weeks. We never quit praying and left it in Almighty God's hands.

My mom hired an attorney. In the eleventh hour, with two arms and a leg already deported back to Columbia, because his sister hadn't filed some paper back in 1966, the Lord Jesus came through for us again! Literally, hours before they were going to deport him, he was set free and acquitted! Check and checkmate! The devil lost his battle against us again!

Then, in February 2006, Eddie, took very ill. He was sick to his stomach, all the time. We figured it was just stress. He worked with a supervisior who was never happy and <u>lived</u> to make everyone else's lives miserable. The devil was making his third and final assault on my husband and I. He wanted us back, on his side, very badly!

During his battle with Immigration, his mom had died. He had been very close to his mother. So, that is why we really thought his illness was stress. **It wasn't**.

The first thing we did, upon realizing Eddie was sick and knowing it was something serious, was fall to our knees, on our faces, before God and confess all of our sins. We spent hours crying out to God, asking Him to show us if there was any unconfessed sins in our lives. We knew we were under attack from the devil and we knew we needed to hold on tighter, to the Lord, than ever before. We knew we couldn't turn to the right or to the left even a little. We needed to stay on the straight and narrow path and stay as close, to the Lord, as humanly possible.

We sent him to doctor after doctor. He was taking Alka Seltzer four or five times a day. We sent him to the best internal medicine doctor in our area, who had been in practice, probably, 30 years. He did tests, but he had no clue. He should have known. Eddie's general practitioner thought he was a diabetic and looked no further. We were beyond frustrated.

Eddie kept losing weight, rapidly. Of course, because he couldn't keep anything down. We were **desperate** to find an answer. I knew if we didn't, I was going to lose him and never know why.

A friend of ours told us about a herbal doctor in a near by city. He called to make an appointment and found out she didn't take insurance, only cash. God only knows how we came up with the money, but we did. The doctor told him he had something wrong with his pancreas and that it was serious. Then, she hugged him.

As soon, as he told me what the doctor had said, I said, "Oh, My God! Help us!" I felt like I had been hit in the stomach and had the wind knocked out of me.

She gave him herbs to take to clean out his system, but, it was total unbearable and made the problem much worse.

She told him to come back in two weeks, but we couldn't get another $150.00 together. I begged him to go to the hospital. He wouldn't go, because his father had died in a hospital. I cried and begged, but still he wouldn't go.

We reached out and held on very tightly to the Lord Jesus' hand and His Word. There was nothing else we could do. We were trying everything we knew to do, and it wasn't good enough. I stood there watching him die and was helpless to do anything else for him.

Still, my Eddie who had been about 190 pounds in February was now, in September, at about 150 and dropping.

On New Years Eve, 2006, jaundice and to weak to argue with me any further, I **forced** him to go to the hospital. They couldn't believe how horrible he looked. They didn't make him sit in the waiting room at all. They took him ahead of everyone else.

Everyone we knew had been praying for us, all these months. His family and mine are strong believers. So, the first call I made was to my sister. Her faith surpasses anyone I have ever known. She and her husband of 34 years were on a rare date night. They dropped everything and rushed to the hospital to be with me. We cried and prayed together. We couldn't read the Word, for our tears, but my sister, Brenda, kept bringing to mind verses she had memorized. I couldn't have told you my name, at that point. Together, we called our other family members, and his family in New York and Cape Coral. They continued to pray and cried with me.

Three hours later, at 10:00 pm, they called me in to be with Eddie. He took me in his arms and held me, very close. Then, as he held my hands he told me, "They think I have Cancer." I sobbed uncontrobablly. All the signs had been there, but we had missed them. Why, had all these doctors not seen it? They ask me to leave and followed me out into the hallway. The doctor said to me, very matter of fact,

"He has pancreatic cancer and he isn't going to make it through the night."

Without thinking, I responded, **"Oh, yes he will! Because doctors don't have the last say, God does. And we belong to Him!"** She thought I was just in denial. I said to myself, **"Let's just stand back and watch God work a miracle!"**

Our very strong faith had brought us through so many things in our lives, we were not about to change course now.

Over the next few days, through test after horrible test, and more and more blood work, not one medical person was encouraging. They all kept saying the same thing, 'He isn't going to make it.' My sister barely left my side. My mom had taken ill, so she and my dad couldn't come to be with me, but they kept calling to check on Eddie. My daughters, Eddie's step-children, got time off from work and came to be with me. To say the future was bleak would be a total understatement. But, we kept holding on securely to our faith.

What are you going through? Are **you** holding tightly to the hand of Jesus?

I had been a Christian 37 years at that point. Did I believe everything I had studied and learned over that time or not?

When it comes right down to it, do you really believe Jesus is capable of taking care of everything in your life?

I think it was at this time that God gave me a vision. My sister, Eddie and I and the Lord Jesus were in a straight line, side by side. Our arms were linked together for strength and we were walking down a wide paved road with tall trees on either side. Down, meaning literally down, a hill into a deep, deep valley. We knew it was going to be a very rough ride and continued to pray for Jesus' help to get us through. We knew it was completely hopeless, without Him. Just the sweet name of Jesus brought us comfort, just His name. His Word was like gold to us, it was that precious. We grabbed hold of Psalms 37:1-8 and would not let go. The Word came to life, or so it seemed, and time after time we were shown verses we didn't even know were there. The Lord continued to comfort us with His Word.

We determined, that no matter what, we would continue to praise the Lord and glorify Him. We were going to tell anyone, who would listen, about Jesus and His saving Grace.

We went boldly before the throne of God, and ask for a miracle.

What was the worst that could happen? God could tell us no.

Hebrews 4:16 KJV: *"Let us therefore come boldly unto the throne of grace, that we may obtain mercy, and find grace to help in time of need."*

I kept claiming the verse in:

Isaiah 53:5 KJV: *"With His stripes we are healed."*

I didn't even know if that meant physical healing, but I claimed it anyway. The Lord kept bringing these verses to me over and over again.

Matthew 9:20-21 KJV: *"And, behold, a woman, which was diseased with an issue of blood twelve years, came behind Him, and touched the hem of His garment: For she said within herself, If I may but touch his garment, I shall be whole."*

The Holy Spirit showed me that the **ONLY** way she could touch the hem of His garment, would be if she was kneeling at His feet. I kneeled often, humbly before the Lord and cried out to Him for mercy on my husband.

They told us we needed to go to another hospital, with more experienced doctors in this field. Are they kidding? He could barely move. Everytime he took a breath I shuttered, thinking, for sure, it was going to be his last. Yet, they wanted me to move him halfway across the state to another hospital, in fact, almost to Georgia from Southwest Florida?

"Ok," I said, "whatever we have to do. So, you are going to fly him there, right? Or take him by ambulance?" No, both were $3,000.00 and the insurance only paid $1,500.00 of that. I needed the rest in cash. It might as well been a million. I barely had gas money.

"He will never make it," we thought to ourselves, but never verbalize it. But, we all knew it, including Eddie.

So, knowing The Lord will never leave us or forsake us, my sister and I put my extremely ill husband, in our van and drove him to Gainesville, in the dark. Armed with a map quest map and a prayer, we headed out, on a starless night. I was exhausted and had only a vague idea where the hospital was. Even, as a seasoned courier, I was scared to death! The devil thought he had us defeated. But, **he didn't**! We never stopped praying and when the torrential rain started, my sister and I started singing and quoting verses even louder. Eddie yelled from the backseat, "I am in enough pain already! Quit singing." We laughed knowing he was joking and that was his way of dealing with the utter fear that possessed every grain of his being. **We refused to be defeated.** We knew the devil was on the offense, so we held our faith together for a stronger defense. Our Captain was the Lord Jesus and He was on our side. Who can defeat us with that line up? No one!

It was midnight on January 5, 2007, when we arrived at the emergency room at Shands Hospital in Gainesville, Florida. It was freezing cold. To keep ourselves occupied and our minds off of Eddie, my sister took out a tablet and started writing down prayer requests. We never realized, at that time, that we were adding to our own *spiritual suitcases* with every word we uttered and every prayer we prayed.

Eight hours later, they finally took him back to a room. We had not eaten or slept in many, many hours. Yet, my hypoglycemic didn't kick in. We had only a drinking fountain and cold sodas from the machine. Yet, we were all ok.

Finally, after another three hours, they reluctantly, admitted him. They thought he was going to die, and didn't see the sense in wasting their time. I figured, they did not want to be held responsible. I wanted to scream, "Just help him!"

Time after time, they looked at the records we had brought and repeated the same tests again. No one could believe he was still alive. But, the three of us just kept claiming the name of Jesus over the situation. We held hands and prayed over him.

Finally, they decided they could help him. One doctor even told us, "This is totally curable." We knew that wasn't true. Jesus was as close to us, as our skin. No kidding.

After one week, they sent him home to regain his strength. Again, we couldn't believe they were releasing him. A week later, we returned and they did more tests and prepared him for surgery. They told us, it was a **total** long shot that he was even going to make it through the surgery. They said not to get our hopes up and told him to make his peace with God. We just kept saying, "It's in God's hands, not ours." But, inwardly, I prepared myself for the worst.

As we waited, my sister and I, prayed and cried. We prayed, with other hurting people and told them about God's love and comfort for them. We talked of His salvation, but mainly that Jesus is always with us. We just kept worshipping Jesus and praising His Holy name for bringing us this far.

The doctors did the first surgery. We were to wait in the waiting room. They told us it would take eight hours. After an hour and half, they called us to the waiting room upstairs. We were sure he was dead. I couldn't quit crying. The doctor, a 35 year veteran in this type of surgery, told us he had never seen such a large tumor. He assured us Eddie was alive, but told us they couldn't remove the tumor, in his pancreas, without killing him, because the blood vessels were already intertwined around the tumor. The tumor was to big for the doctors, but **NOTHING** is to big for God. They gave him two months to live. I refused to accept it, because I hadn't heard from God yet.

I had been on the phone, with several of Eddie's family members. Many of them came to be with us. His sisters Maria and Grace flew in from New York. His sister, Judy came from the East Coast of Florida, near Ft Lauderdale. His brother, Richie and his sister Betty came with their families from Cape Coral, Florida. Many of his nieces and nephews said whatever I needed to just call.

Many times our families joined our hands, together with nurses, orderlies and other hospital personnel, in prayer over Eddie's bed. He joined his faith with ours. We held prayer meetings and Bible studies, in his room, and the staff and other people would join us, as we continued to worship the Lord and pray for healing.

Eddie was very scared, as we all were, but we held on strong to our powerful faith, and kept praying.

Luke 22:42 KJV: *"nevertheless not my will, but thine, be done."*

We didn't want to pray that one. This has to be the toughest verse in the Bible. We wanted him to be healed, **now**. Brenda kept up an unending recitation of verses to encourage us. Psalms 37:1-8 says, Fret not, three times.

Psalm 37:4 & 7 NIV: became a verse we kept quoting to encourage ourselves. *"Delight yourself in the Lord and he will give you the desires of your heart." "Be still before the Lord and wait patiently for Him; do not fret--."*

He did indeed make it through, just as my faith had led me to say that first night. He had came through the surgery, but we were still holding our breath, as to rather he would make it very long. It was like waiting for the other shoe to drop. I was afraid to take a deep breath. In other words, I could only handle a little bit of reality at a time.

After two weeks, they sent him home. His family and mine took turns watching him while I returned to work, so I could pay the ever mounting bills. They cooked for him and bought him new clothes and so many kept sending money again and again. They took him to doctor appointments and rushed him back to the hospital when his stitches opened up. He complained that they were hovering over him, but out of love.

He started going for chemotherapy and radiation. The doctors and staff were beyond excellent and compassionate. When our insurance ran out and we were switching to Medicaid there was a lapse of a week or so. He needed the medicine for that time and it was about $1,500.00. We didn't have even close to that. His doctor gave him the medicine and never charged us! That was another miracle!

My youngest daughter, one of Eddie's step children (Eddie and I married when we were both 49) refused to get married, until Eddie was well enough to walk her down the aisle. On May 4, 2007, he was able to do just that and make both of their dreams come true. He had only sons and he thought of Kristin as his daughter.

In the fall of 2007, his cancer doctor, in Cape Coral, declared him CANCER FREE! We were telling everyone we saw about the power of God. **We had gotten our miracle!**

In October 2007, Eddie was strong enough to walk in the *Relay for Life Cancer Walkathon.*

In January 2008, after many months of radiation, chemotherapy and two surgeries, his doctors in Gainesville, declared him **Cancer free**! Wherever we went, everyone who had seen or heard about the journey, marveled at God's miracle of healing my husband. It was a miracle he had made it through the first night!

We praised God! Many people saw the power of God through this difficult journey, we had come through. We had known, from the beginning, we were being tested, to ready us, to minister to others and tell them about Jesus. We had prayed that we would be found to be faithful and indeed, we were. Even non-believers marveled, not at us, but at the power of God to bring someone through this.

I wish I could end the testimony there, but I can't. At every turn or change of events, the devil **thought** he could mess with two of God's children. **He couldn't!**

The reason he can't, is because on the cross, Jesus said, "It is finished." That means He has fought the battle on our behalf and He (Jesus) has won! Enough already! It is finished! Glory be to God!

But, in April 2008, the devil thought he'd try one more time. He is persistent. He knew that both of us had been huge sinners, in the past, and he kept trying to get us to turn back, **but we never did**! Thank you, Jesus!

Eddie started having severe pains in his back. He went directly to the hospital. The cancer had returned at stage four and this time had settled in his liver. There was nothing they could do. No treatment could stop it's rapid advance and two months later, on June 29, 2008, at 1:00 pm, he succumb to this final battle. The devil thought, **'I've won!'** Again, he was wrong and oh, how wrong he was!

The instant my husband passed into glory, a big smile came to his lips and we knew he had just seen Jesus! **The ultimate victory is ours!** The devil loses, Jesus wins, **every** time! Check and checkmate! **And because Jesus wins, so do we!** Praise be to God! When Jesus said it is finished, it meant He has the final say. You, too, can have victory over the devil.

James 4:7-8 NIV: *"Resist the devil, and he will flee from you. Come near to God and He will come near to you."*

Use the Word of God to fight the devil. Use your Shield of faith to stop those firey darts he shoots at us. Put on your whole armor and get ready for battle! Lead with your Shield and have your Sword of the Spirit ready to use against your enemies. You can lead others to Jesus! He will help you. Ready, set, go! The lost world is waiting for you to show them the way to Heaven.

Will you take the challenge or not?

NOTES

Psalms 23 KJV: *"The Lord is my shepherd; I shall not want. He maketh me to lie down in green pastures: he leadeth me beside the still waters. He restoreth my soul: he leadeth me in the paths of righteousness for his name's sake. Yea, though I walk through the valley of the shadow of death, I will fear no evil: for thou art with me; thy rod and thy staff they comfort me. Thou prepares a table before me in the presence of mine enemies: thou anointest my head with oil; my cup runneth over. Surely goodness and mercy shall follow me all the days of my life: and I will dwell in the house of the Lord for ever."* **Amen and Amen**

— Summary —

Every day, you should be packing or unpacking something in your **spiritual suitcase.** You should be packing things like, leading others to Jesus, helping someone in need, or forgiving someone who has done you wrong. Or unpacking things like bitterness, being judgmental, or angry, not just once in awhile, but every day. Have you told anyone, today, that there is a God who loves them so much, that He sacrificed His own Son for the forgiveness of their sins? Have you ask anyone, today, "May I pray with you" and meant it?

How much more could you add to your **spiritual suitcase** and to the Kingdom of God, if you tried a little more to complete the mission God has given you? Let's all try harder today, won't you?

I Peter 5:6-7 KJV: *"Humble yourselves therefore under the mighty hand of God, that He may exalt you in due time: Casting all your care upon Him; for He careth for you."* He is right there with you! He isn't going to leave you to your own devices.

Hold on tight! Do not wavier from the straight path! Read your Bible, pray and confess your sins to Him, daily! Unpack sin from your suitcase, daily!

I Thessalonians 5:17 KJV: *"Pray without ceasing!"*

Pray for each other, not for what you will receive back from them, but because you love them in the Lord. Pack your **spiritual** *suitcase* daily! Too many Christians are sitting on the shelf and doing NOTHING for Jesus. Don't be one of them!

Trust Him with your life, your money and your time. You will be rewarded for your faithfulness! Use those Spiritual gifts to the glory of the Lord, constantly! Worship and praise Him, continually! Tell the lost! Tell them! Tell your family. Tell your friends. Tell your co-workers. Tell them today that Jesus is Lord. Don't wait until tomorrow, because that could be to late.

II Thessalonians 2:12 NIV: says; *"and so that all will be condemned who have not believed the truth but have delighted in wickedness."*

II Corinthians 6:2 KJV: *"in the day of salvation have I succoured thee: behold now is the acceptable time; behold, now is the day of salvation."*

Philippians 2:9-11 NIV: *"Therefore God exalted Him to the highest place and gave Him the name that is above every name, that at the name of Jesus every knee should bow, in Heaven and on Earth and under the Earth, and every tongue confess that Jesus Christ is Lord, to the glory of God the Father."*

So, imagine again, the open suitcase on your bed. It is ready and waiting to be filled. What are you going to pack inside? Corruption and evil? Or faith in Jesus, love and good works done unto the Lord that will not be burned up at the judgment seat?

NOTES

Your suitcase is still open; it's time to pack your *Spiritual Suitcase!*

What are you going to pack inside?

HIS HAND IS HOLDING MINE

Sometimes it's the valley, God asks me to go through, but He never asks me to go alone, His word is always true, His hand is holding mine, All the way through.

Brenda Keyes Granfield

— *Acknowledgments* —

Strong's Exhaustive Concordance: By James Strong S.T.D., LLD.
Riverside Book and Bible House
Iowa Falls, Iowa 50126

Twelve Months of Sundays: By Miss Nan
Tyndale House Publishers, Inc
Copyright 2008

Women's Devotional Bible: By The Zondervan Corporation
The Zondervan Publishing House
Grand Rapids, Michigan 49506
Copyright 1990
New International Version

The Ryrie Study Bible: Charles Caldwell Ryrie, Th.D., Ph.D.
Copyright by Moody Bible Institute of Chicago 1976 and 1978
King James Bible

New King James Bible: By Thomas Nelson Inc.
Copyright 1974-1994

Bible.com, Inc.
Bible.com Ministries
1995-2005
Excellent source of information!

Cyperspace Ministries.com
Copyright 1995-2005
Their study on Spiritual Gifts was very helpful!

Jeff Ferguson Ministries
Joshua Creek Music
Jeff Ferguson Music
9 Music Square South
Suite 211
Nashville, Tennessee 37203
The words to 'Halfway' were used and permission was granted by
Jeff Ferguson and Angie Whatley

Adrian Rogers
Love Worth Finding Ministries
P.O. Box 38300
Memphis, Tennessee 38183
The use of the phrase "Golden Nuggets" were used with the
permission of his office.

Matthew West Ministries
5409 Maryland Way
Suite 200
Brentwood, Tennessee 37027
Going Through the Motions
Copyright 2009

Greg Laurie Ministries
6115 Arlington Ave.
Riverside, California 92504
The story of the pastor on the beach was used. Permission was granted by Diane at Harvest Christian Fellowship.

Contact information:
PACKING YOUR SPIRITUAL SUITCASE
% Pamela M. Torres or
Brenda Keyes Granfield
17533 Lee Road
Fort Myer, Florida 33967
239-267-7688
239-244-4739

Pamela Keyes Torres and Brenda Keyes Granfield

Ohio born, Brenda Keyes Granfield, has been writing since high school.

She graduated from Fort Myers High School and attended Edison Junior College. She married Larry L. Granfield, they have two children and one grandchild. She has had several articles published in local newspapers and magazines and has self published five books, including *THE ADVENTURES OF TOMMY BEAR, WATER SAFETY*, for young children. Brenda has a degree in child care and has cared for children for over thirty years. Having co-authored *PACKING YOUR SPIRITUAL SUITCASE*, she would now, like to serve The Lord with her writing.

Born in Ohio, Pamela M. Torres, has lived in Southwest Florida for most of the past 40 years. She graduated from Fort Myers High School and went on to Edison Junior College, where she majored in American Literature. She has written many articles, which were published in magazines and newspapers, including the McDonald's corporate office newsletter in Dallas, Texas. *PACKING YOUR SPIRITUAL SUITCASE* is the third book she has co-authored with her twin Sister, Brenda. Her main goal is to serve The Lord in this capacity. When time permits, she enjoys spending time with her two daughters and six grandchildren.